Team Spirit

It's fun to do things together.

SCHOLASTIC

LITERACY PLACE®

Copyright acknowledgments and credits appear on page 152, which constitutes an extension of this copyright page.

Copyright © 1996 by Scholastic Inc.   All rights reserved.   Printed in the U.S.A.
ISBN 0-590-49099-0
2 3 4 5 6 7 8 9 10   23   02 01 00 99 98 97 96 95

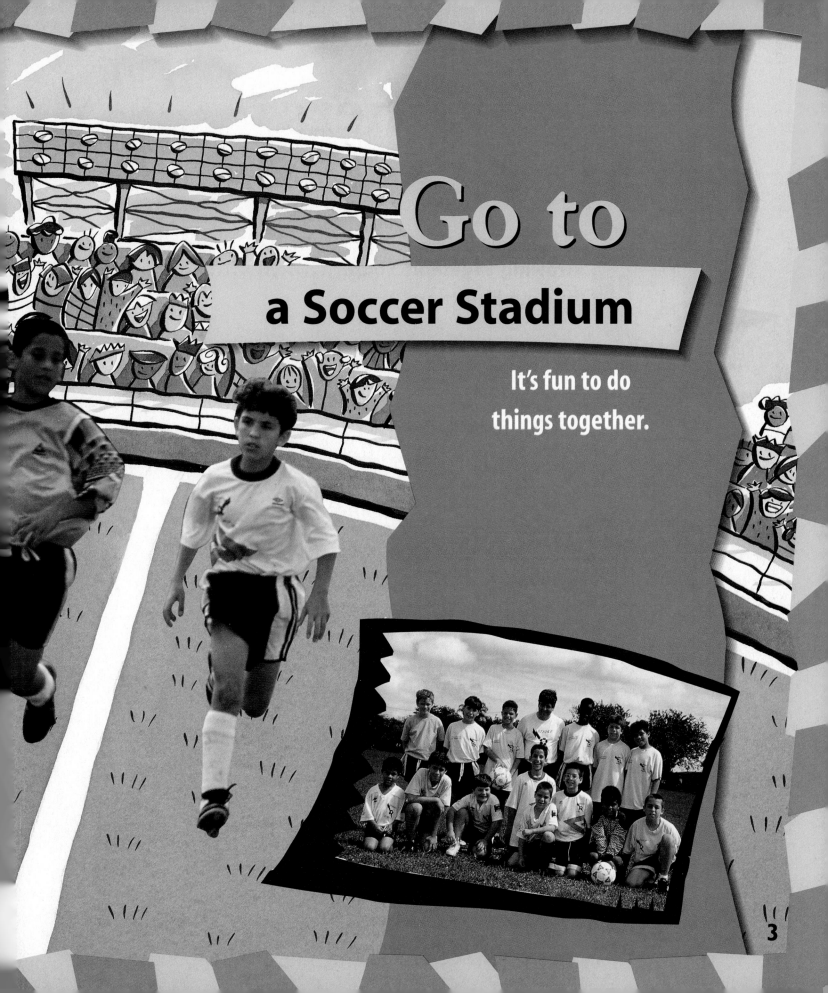

Go to
a Soccer Stadium

It's fun to do
things together.

Partners
Team members work together.

Partners Helping Partners

Sometimes we need help.

Partners at Play

Playing together is fun.

Danny
Prenat

Trade Books

The following books accompany this *Team Spirit* SourceBook.

Nonfiction
This Is Baseball
by Margaret Blackstone
illustrated by John O'Brien

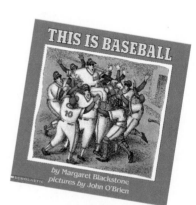

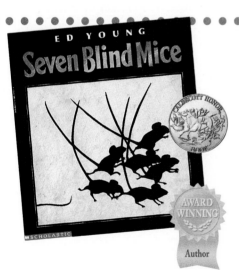

Repetitive Story
The Doorbell Rang
by Pat Hutchins

Cumulative Story
Shoes From Grandpa
by Mem Fox

Big Books

Folk Tale
Seven Blind Mice   Caldecott Honor
by Ed Young

Photo Essay
Loving
by Ann Morris
photographs by Ken Heyman

7

Read Together!

Partners

Team members work together.

Meet a father and child who grow vegetables and turn them into soup.

See how a mom and daughter team up to build a doghouse.

Then see how a grandmother teaches her granddaughter how to make a basket.

Growing Vegetable Soup

AWARD WINNING

Author

Written and illustrated by
Lois Ehlert

Dad says we are going to grow vegetable soup.

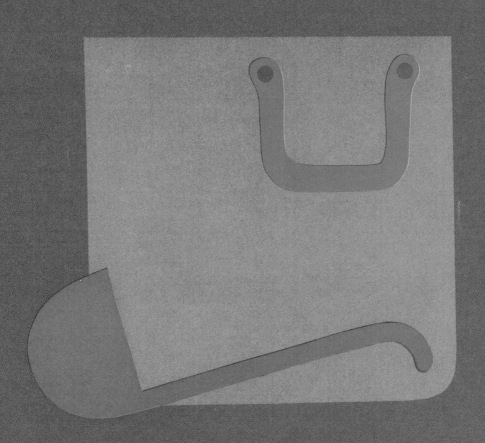

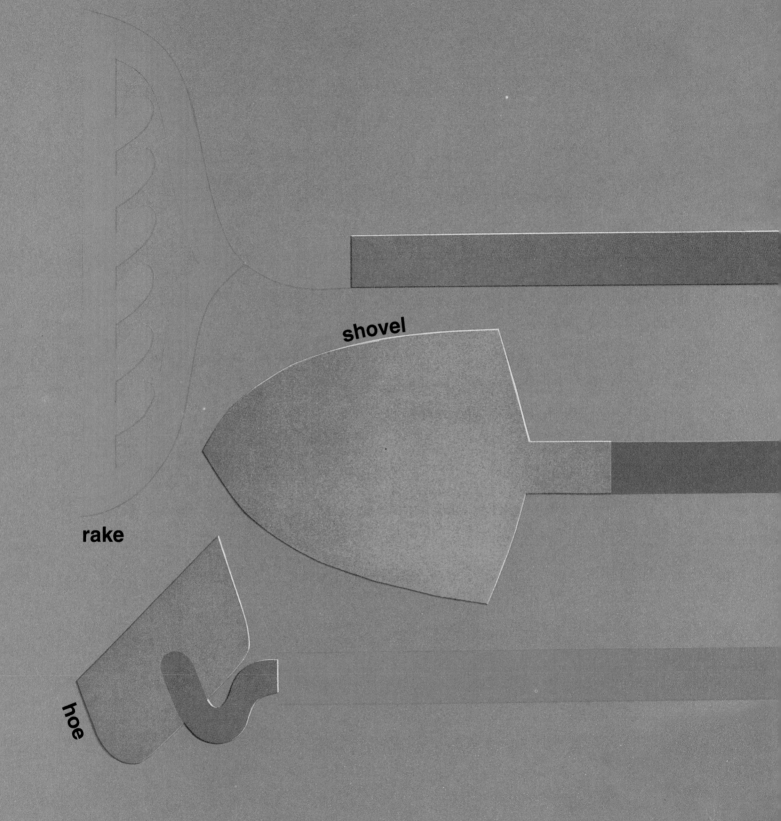

shovel

rake

hoe

12

We're ready to work,

and our tools are

ready, too.

We are planting

seed package

soil

hole

14

the seeds,

garden glove

green bean
seed

pea
seed

corn
seed

zucchini
squash
seed

carrot
seeds

15

and all the sprouts,

broccoli

TOMATO

potato eyes

trowel

PEPPER

CABBAGE

set onions

peat moss pot

17

TOMATO

POTATO

GREEN BEAN

CARROT

CABBAGE

watering can

and giving them water,

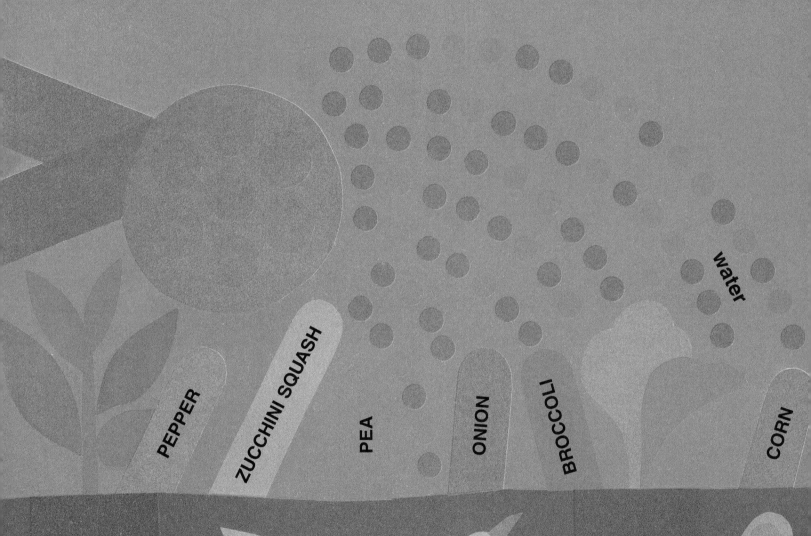

PEPPER

ZUCCHINI SQUASH

PEA

ONION

BROCCOLI

water

CORN

and waiting for warm sun to make them grow,

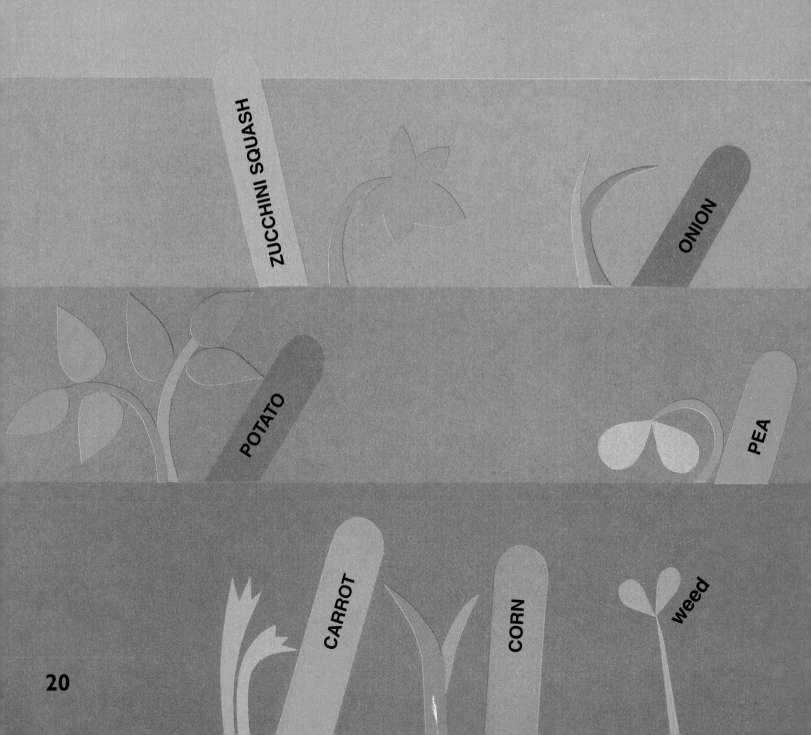

ZUCCHINI SQUASH

ONION

POTATO

PEA

CARROT

CORN

weed

SUN

PEPPER

TOMATO

CABBAGE

GREEN BEAN

BROCCOLI

and grow,

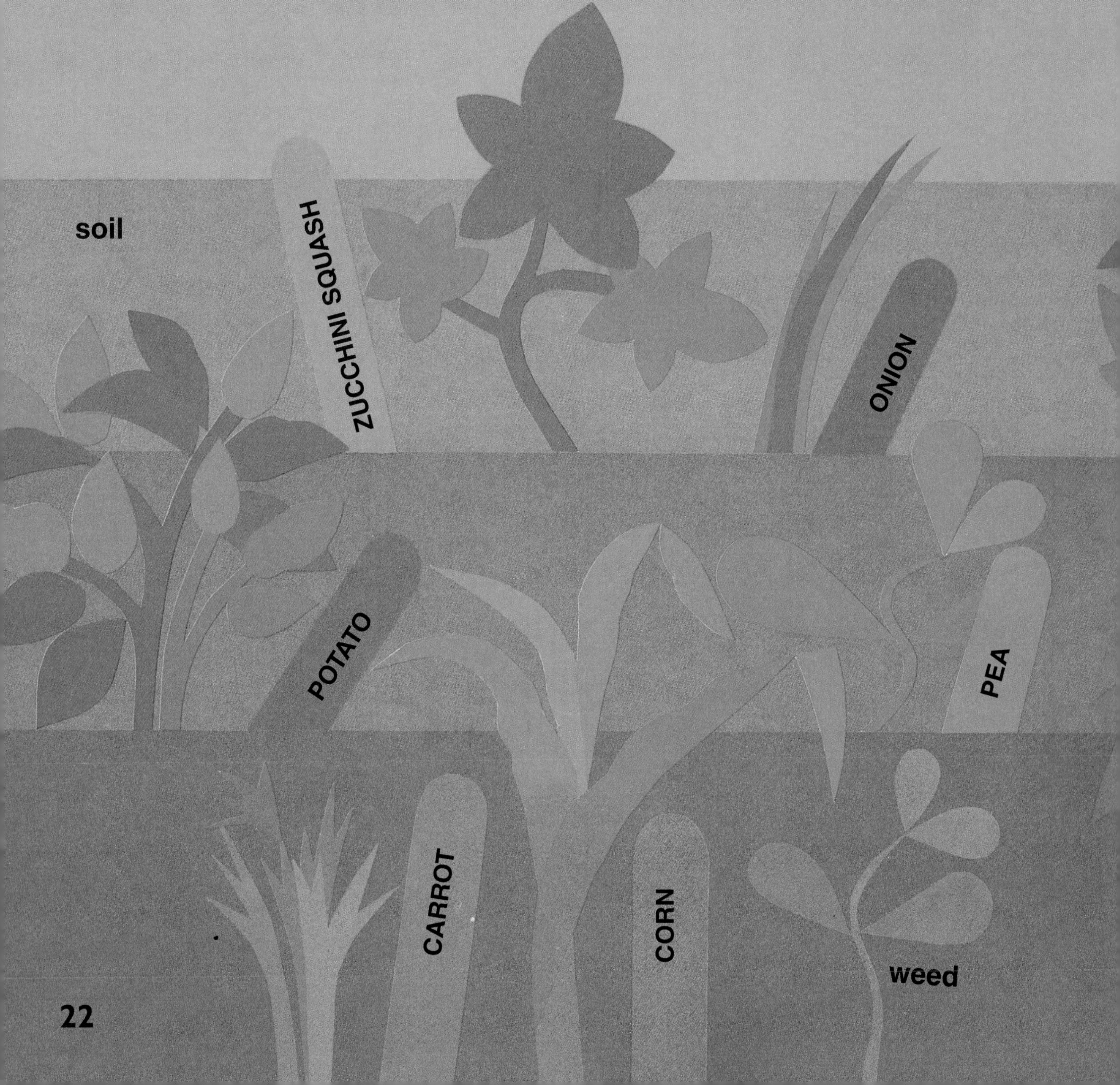

soil

ZUCCHINI SQUASH

ONION

POTATO

PEA

CARROT

CORN

weed

sun

PEPPER

CABBAGE

TOMATO

GREEN BEAN

BROCCOLI

23

and grow into plants.

squash
bud

ZUCCHINI SQUASH

squash
blossom

25

We watch

worm

BROCCOLI

over them and weed,

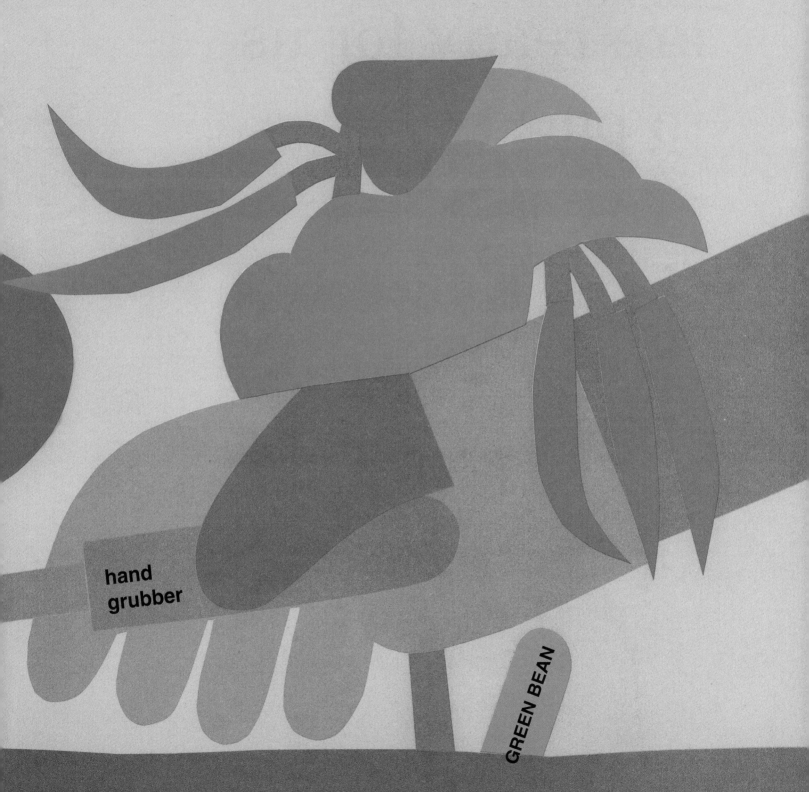

hand
grubber

GREEN BEAN

until the vegetables are ready for us to pick

TOMATO

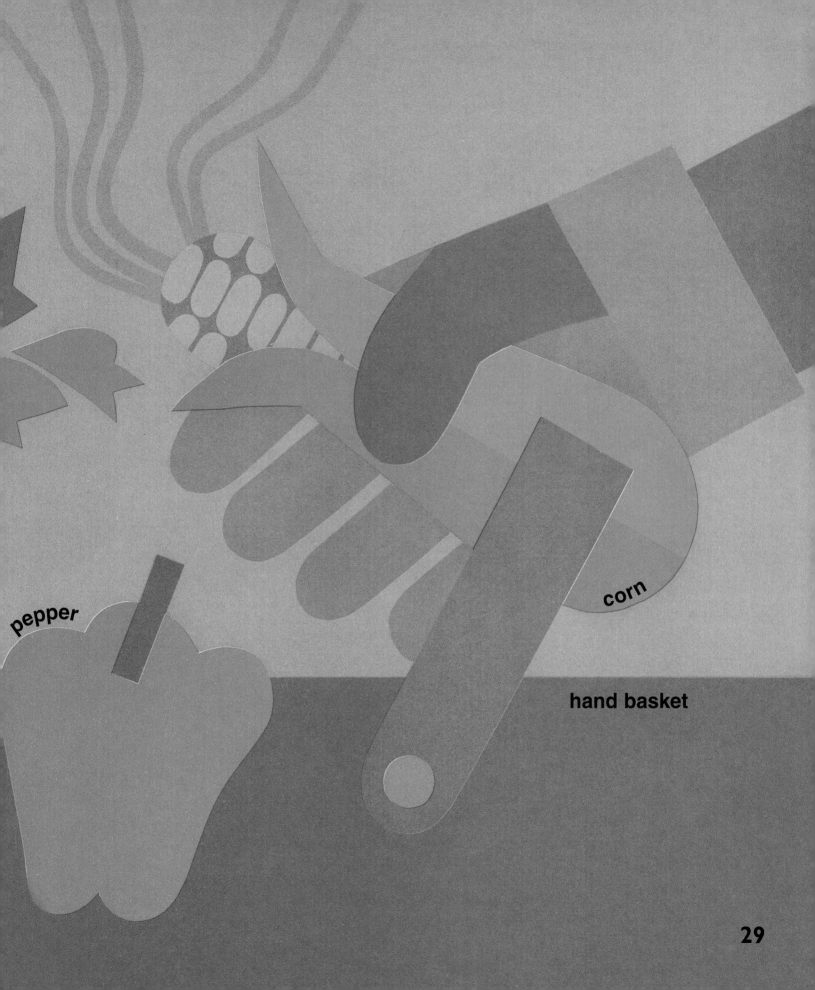

pepper

corn

hand basket

spading
fork

30

or dig up

carrot

potato

bushel basket

and carry home.
Then we wash them

cabbage

onion

pail

and cut them and put them in a pot of water,

soup pot

soup ladle

34

corn

carrot

zucchini squash

onion

tomato

pea

broccoli

potato

pepper

green bean

knife

cabbage

and cook them into vegetable soup!

steam

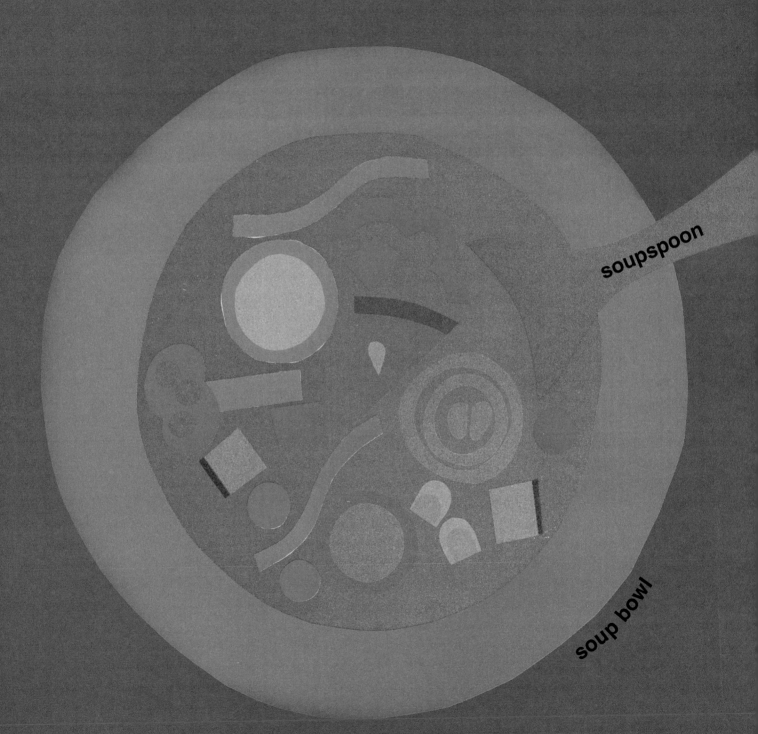

soupspoon

soup bowl

At last it's time
to eat it all up!

It was the best
soup ever...

and we can grow
it again next year.

Harry's House

Written by Angela Shelf Medearis
Illustrated by Susan Keeter

SCHOLASTIC

AWARD WINNING

Author

Momma and I put on overalls.
We're going to build a house
for Harry.

Momma saws the boards.

I sweep up the dust.

Momma hammers in the nails.

I hold the boards for her.

It takes two of us to lift the roof.

To keep the rain out,
we glue tarpaper on the roof.

Momma nails on the shingles.

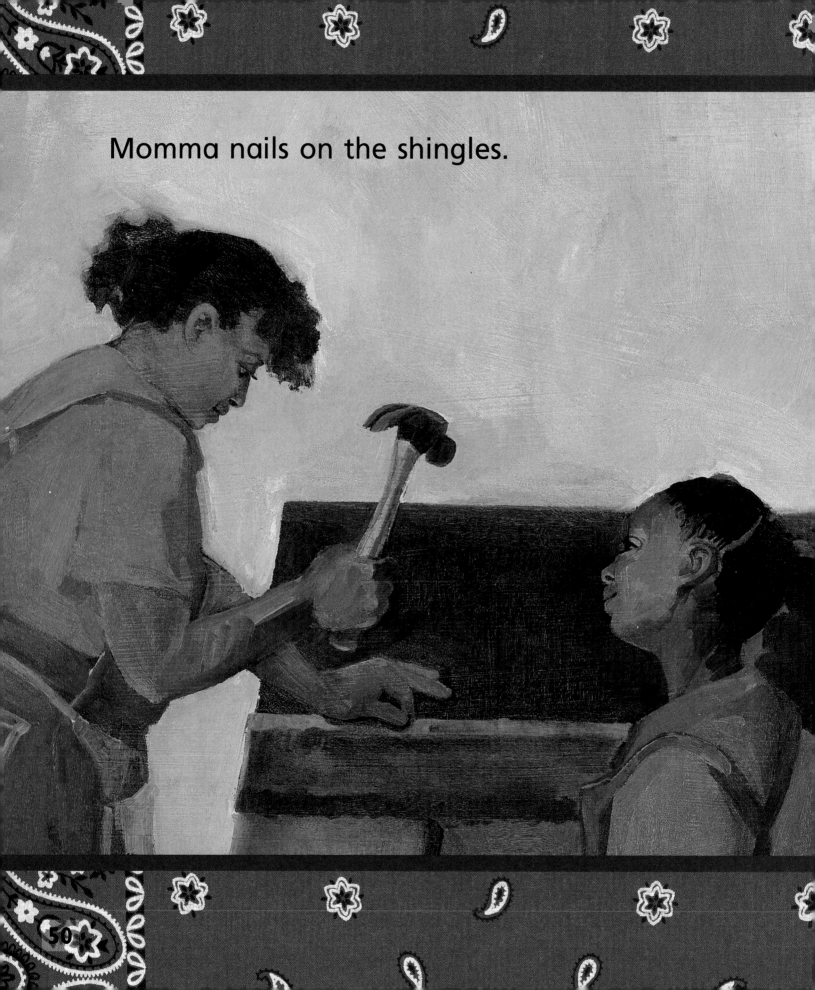

I mix red paint while Momma watches.

Painting is messy work.
But it's fun, too.

Now, Harry's house is all finished.

Good dog, Harry!

Beautiful Baskets

by Diane Hoyt-Goldsmith

My grandmother weaves Cherokee baskets.

First she dips strips of cane in water to make them soft.

Then, she weaves the cane over and under, over and under.

She shows me how she makes beautiful baskets.

Read Together!

Partners Helping Partners

Sometimes we need help.

Read a folk tale about teamwork. Then find out where vegetables grow by reading a chart.

Meet Herman— an octopus who likes to be helpful. Then see how a working dog helps a young boy.

One day, Sione found a huge talo
growing in his garden.

He pulled, and pulled, and pulled,
but he couldn't pull it out.

"E Moka," he called to his wife.
"Come and help me with this talo."

61

They pulled, and pulled, and pulled,
but they couldn't pull it out.

"E Pita," Sione called to his son.
"Come and help us with this talo."

63

They pulled, and pulled, and pulled,
but they couldn't pull it out.

"E Tose," Sione called to his daughter.
"Come and help us with this talo."

65

They pulled, and pulled, and pulled,
but they couldn't pull it out.

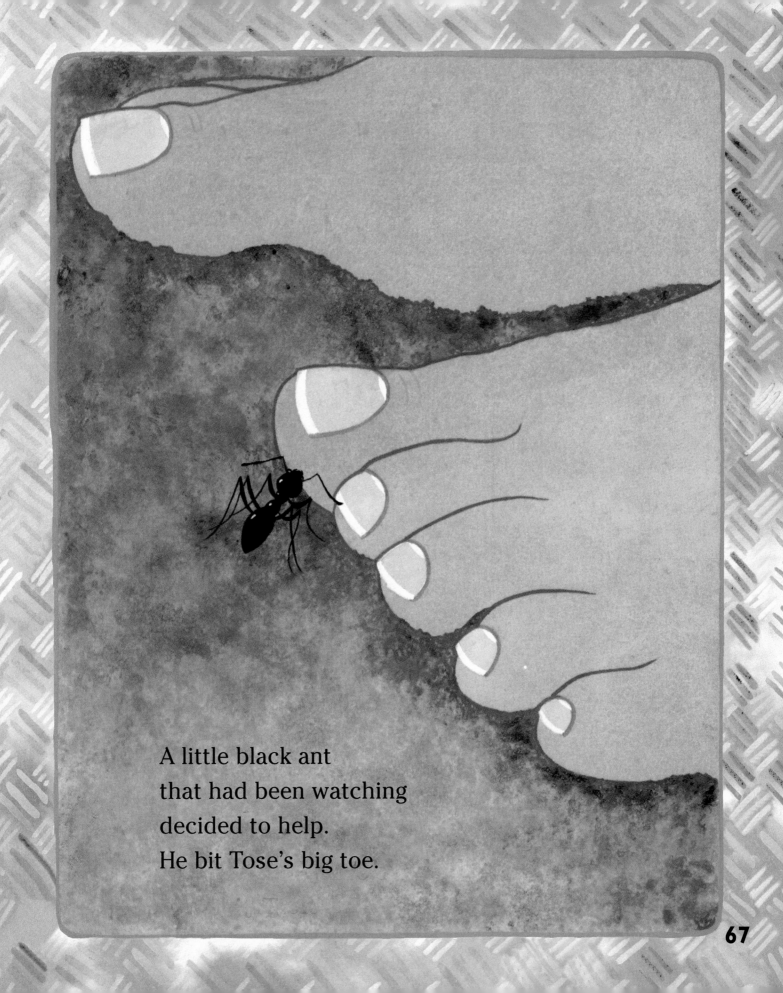

A little black ant
that had been watching
decided to help.
He bit Tose's big toe.

"Oi, oi, oi," cried Tose.
Tose pulled Pita.
Pita pulled Moka.
Moka pulled Sione.
Sione pulled the talo.

Out came the talo
and they all tumbled to the ground.

That night there was enough talo
with coconut cream for everyone to eat.

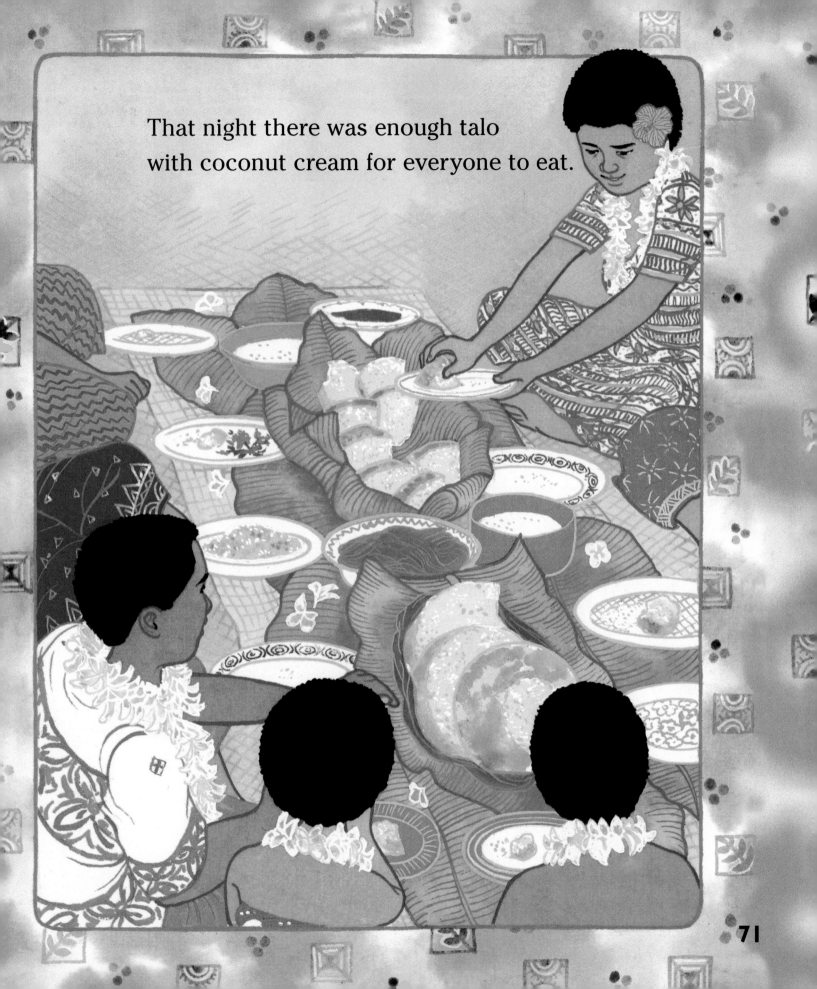

Even enough for the ants.

How Does Your Garden Grow?

Vegetable	Does it grow above or below ground?	The part of the plant you eat
peas	above	seeds
carrot	below	stem
lettuce	above	leaf
potato	below	stem
corn	above	seeds
beet	below	root
 celery	above	stem

73

Herman the Helper

BY ROBERT KRAUS   PICTURES BY JOSE ARUEGO
& ARIANE DEWEY

AWARD
WINNING

Book

Herman liked to help.

Thank you, Herman.

He helped his mother.

That's nice, Herman.

He helped his father.

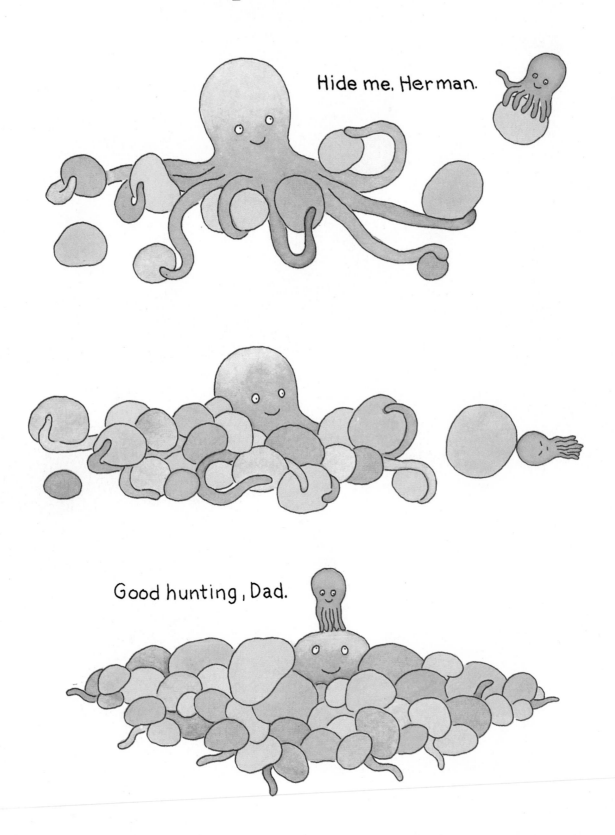

Hide me, Herman.

Good hunting, Dad.

78

That's my dad.

He helped his brothers and sisters.

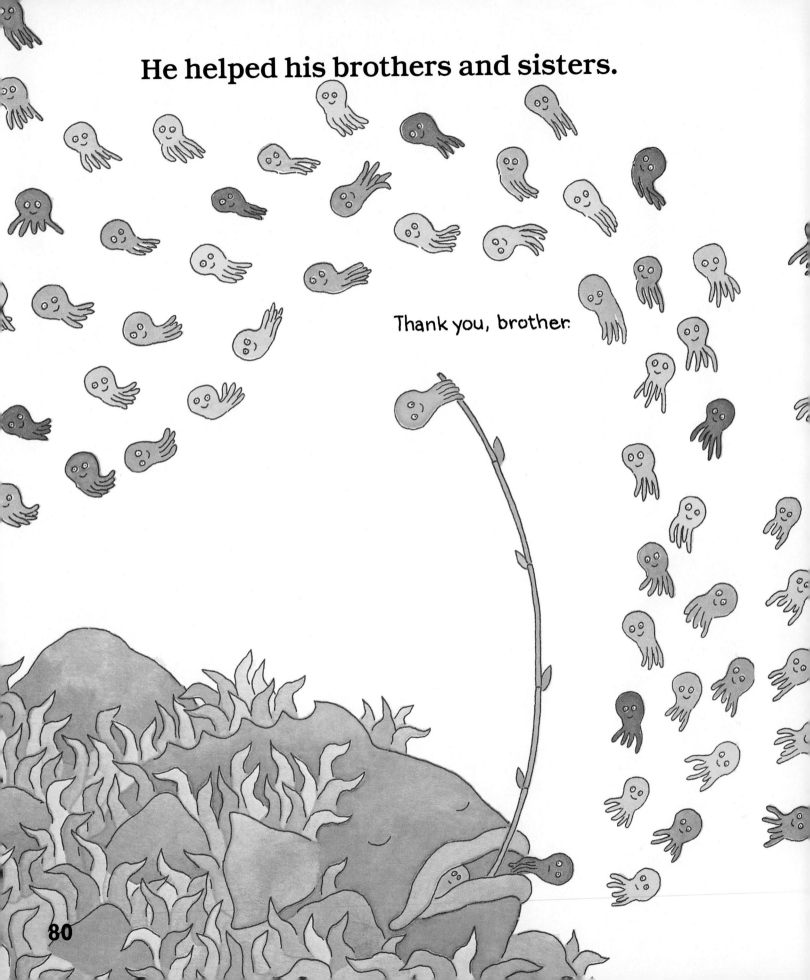

Thank you, brother.

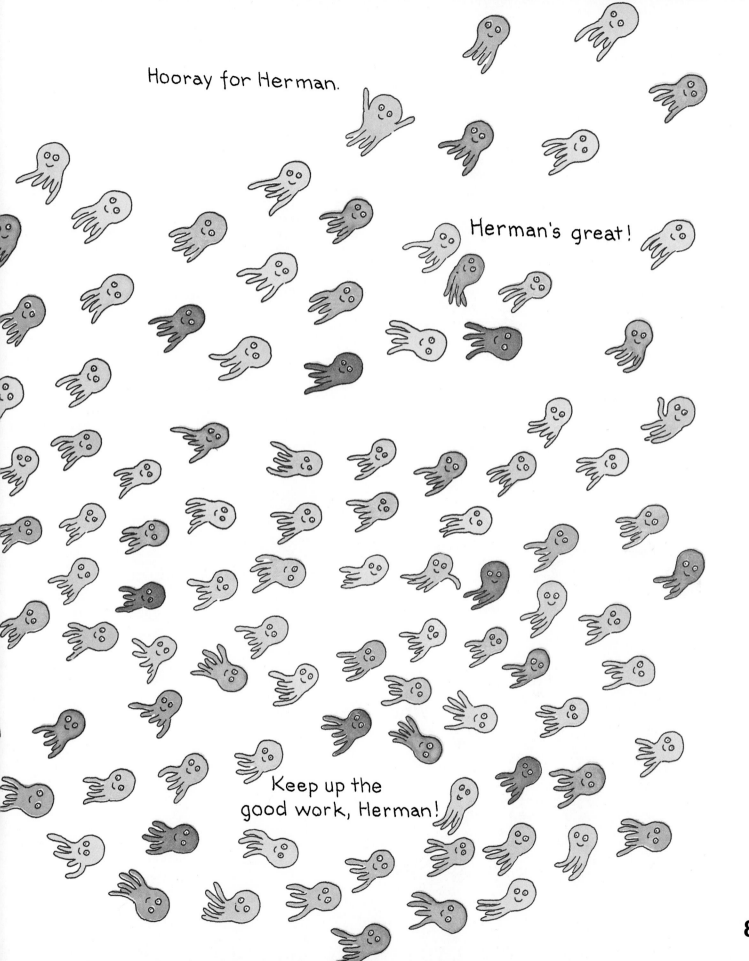

He helped his aunt.

What a beautiful bonnet, Herman.

Yes.

82

He helped his uncle.

He helped his friends.

Many thanks, Herman.

He helped his enemies.

Okay.

Help! It's after us!

I'll camouflage you with my ink.

sisssssssss

Herman saved the day!

He helped the young.

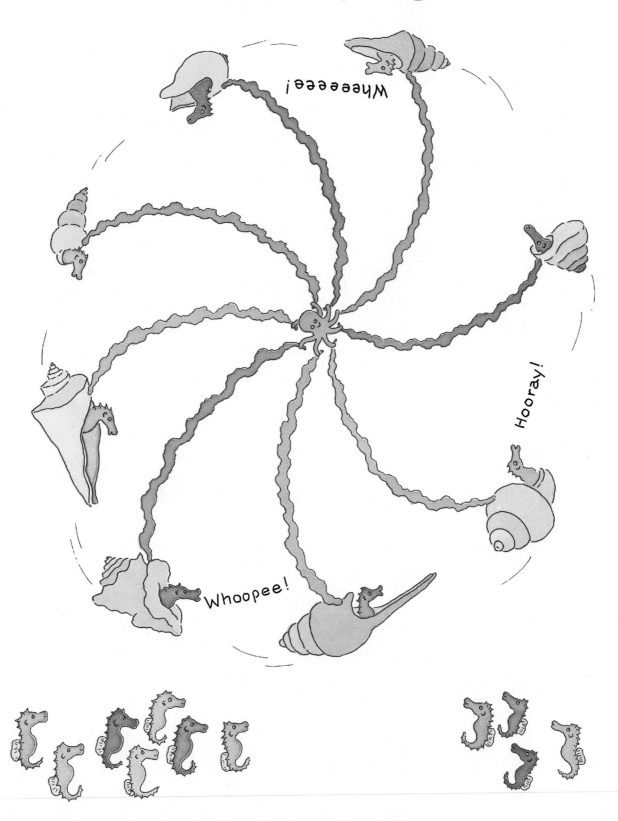

He helped the old.

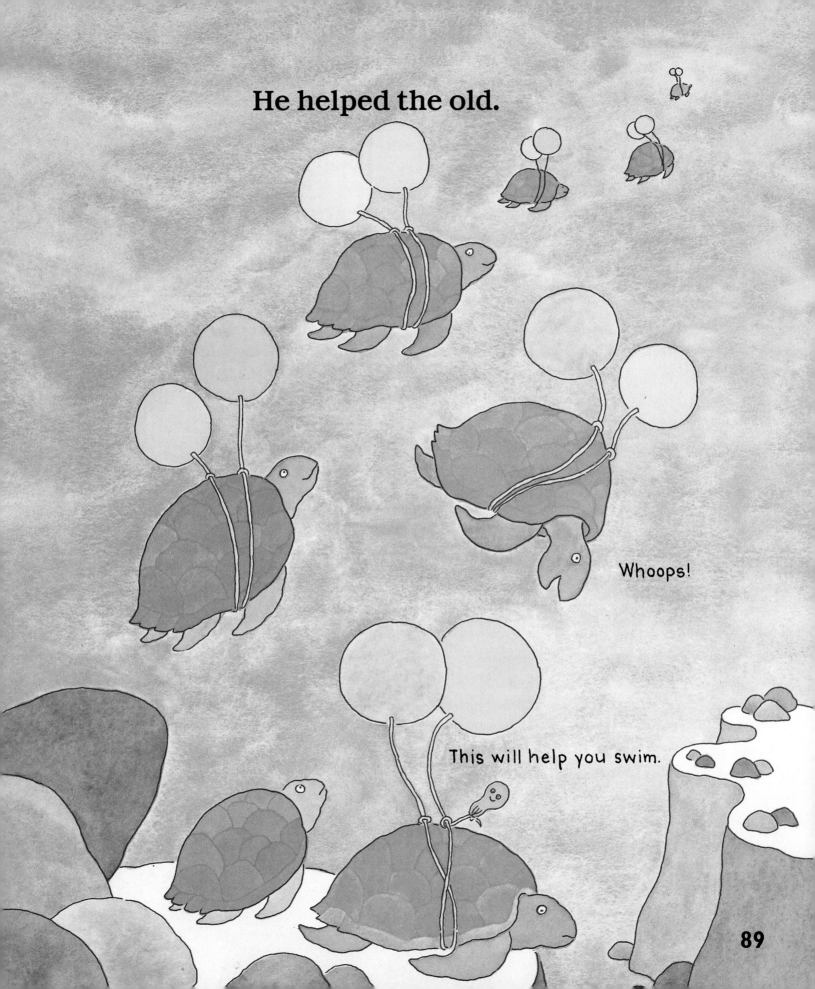

Whoops!

This will help you swim.

He helped the poor and needy.

Our home is beautiful now.

Thanks to Herman.

He helped the fireman.

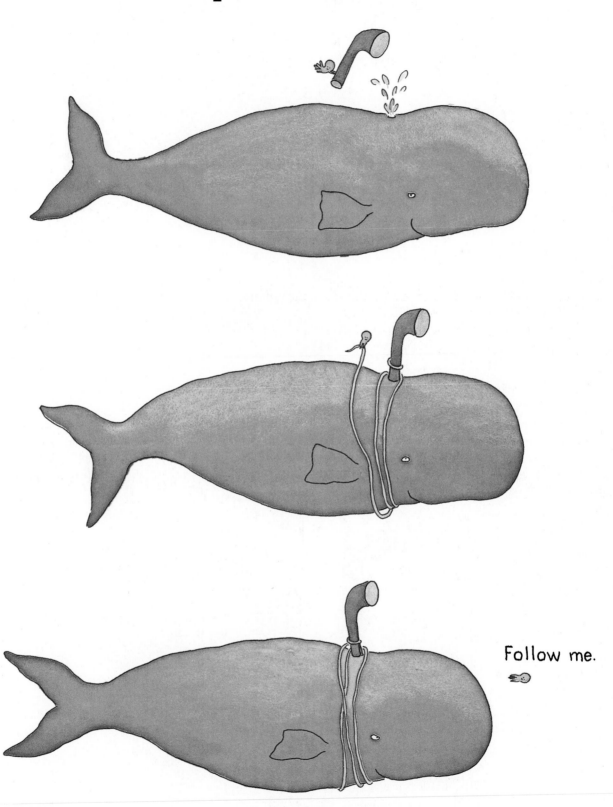

Follow me.

He helped the policeman.

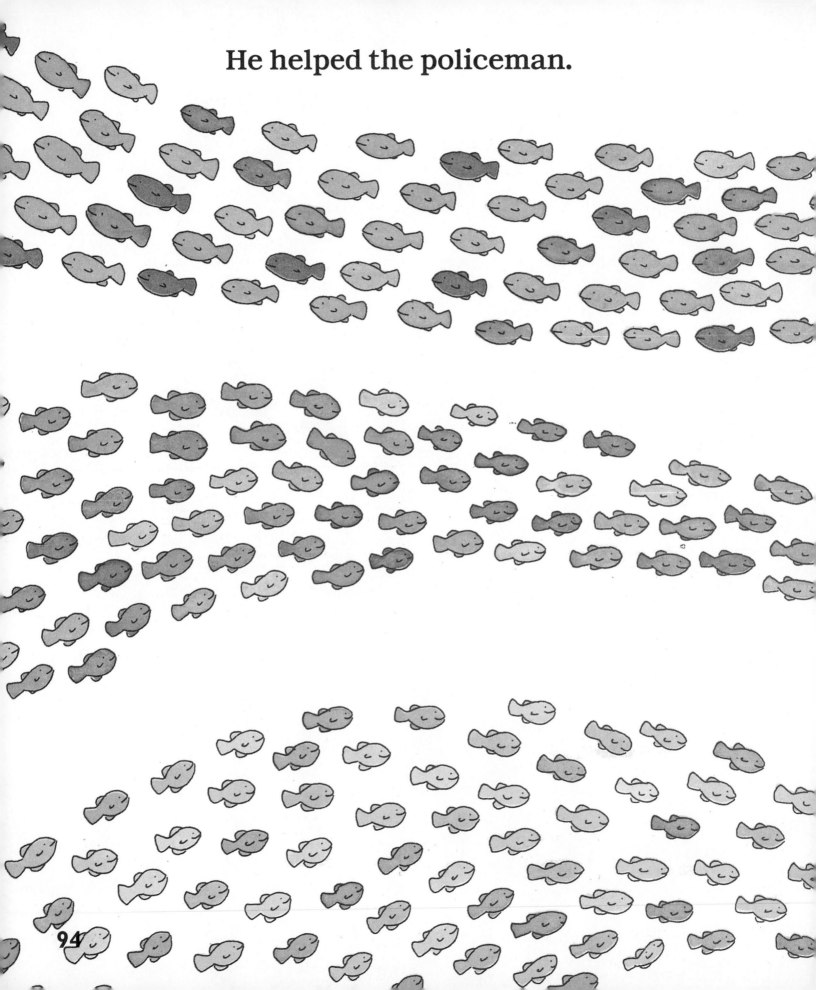

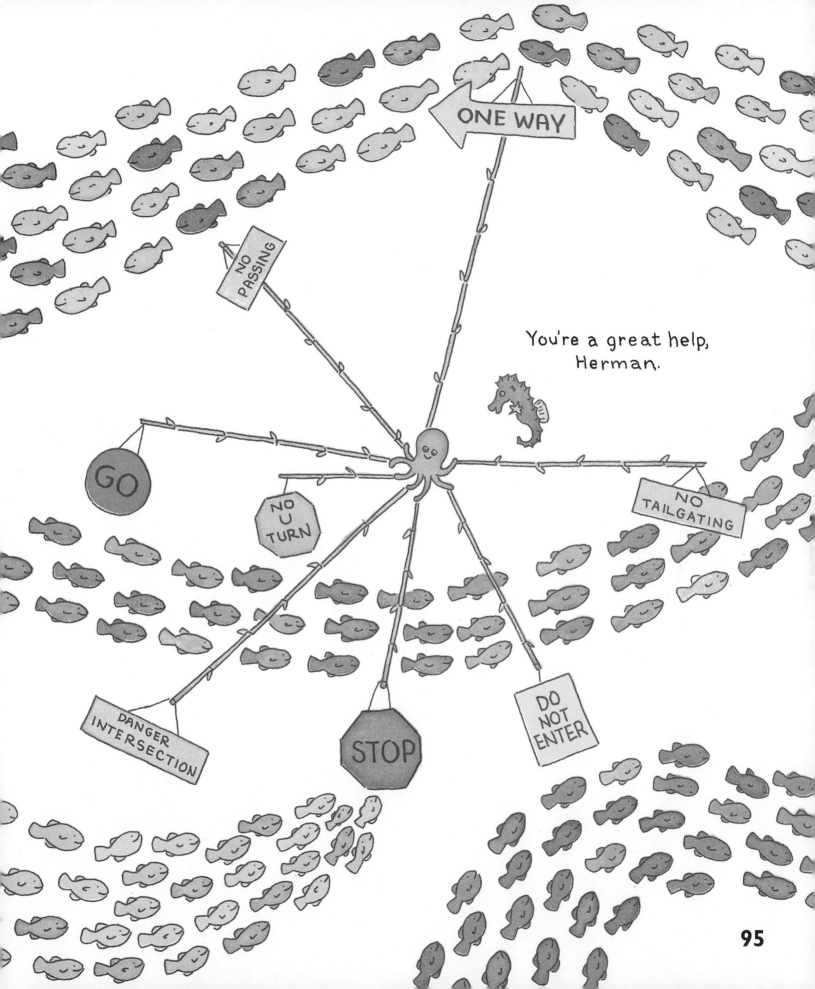

Then the clock struck six and Herman hurried home.

Six o'clock already?

He washed his hands and face.

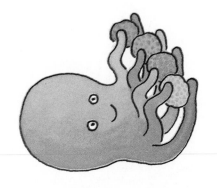

I'm hungry!

And sat down to supper.

"May I help you to some mashed potatoes?"
asked Herman's father.

"No, thanks,"
said Herman.
"I'll help myself."

Thank you,
Herman.

ᵔ We Go ᵔ Together

Kris and his dog Ivy are best friends. They do everything together. Ivy even goes to school with Kris. She carries his books and his lunch.

Kris helps Ivy, too. He feeds her and makes sure she gets to run. They take good care of each other!

SOURCE

SCHOLASTIC NEWS.

News Magazine

Read Together!

Partners at Play

Playing together is fun.

See how many different ways bunnies have fun playing together. Then read a poem about playing jump rope.

Meet a soccer coach who knows what teamwork means.

Learn about the game of soccer.

105

BUNNIES
and Their Sports

BY NANCY CARLSON

BUNNIES AND THEIR SPORTS

CARLSON

VIKING KESTREL

AWARD
WINNING

Author

Every morning when bunnies wake up from
a good night's rest...

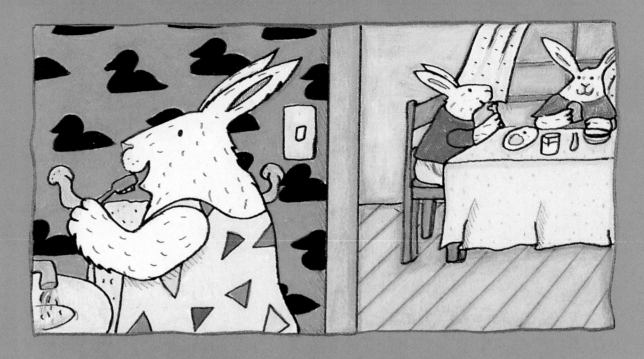

they brush their teeth, eat their breakfast,

and warm up.

Then it's time for bunnies and their sports!!!

Some bunnies like to jog...

others like to hike.

There are swimmer bunnies,

and bunnies who do swan dives.

Competitive bunnies like to play softball,

or touch football.

There are waterskiing bunnies,

and there are snow bunnies.

Sometimes many bunnies gather together

for a game of volleyball....

Brave bunnies go surfing,

or climb high mountains.

There are bunnies who go to gyms...

to lift weights,

...play basketball,

or do aerobics.

There are bunnies who roller-skate,

and bunnies who ice-skate.

Some bunnies like to exercise quietly by doing yoga,

or scuba diving deep underwater.

Some bunnies exercise outdoors, playing soccer, biking,

or playing tennis!!

Different bunnies like

different sports...

but all bunnies do sports because
they make them feel good!!!

Read Together!

ROPE RHYME

by Eloise Greenfield
illustrated by Diane and Leo Dillon

Get set, ready now, jump right in
Bounce and kick and giggle and spin
Listen to the rope when it hits the ground
Listen to that clappedy-slappedy sound
Jump right up when it tells you to
Come back down, whatever you do
Count to a hundred, count by ten
Start to count all over again
That's what jumping is all about
Get set, ready now,
                    jump
                        right
                            out!

135

Danny Prenat

Soccer Coach

Danny Prenat coaches young people in Florida. He shows them how to work as a team.

● Soccer players learn the rules and how to pass the ball.

● Players practice what they learn on the field.

"Players need to be a team," Coach Prenat says. "They learn to work together. Good teams have fun."

Soccer Is Our Game

by Leila Boyle Gemme

Soccer is our game.
We like to run and kick.
We learn to kick.
Our hands may not
touch the ball.

Our coach shows us how to kick.
We have to dribble the ball.
It is fun to make short kicks.

We pass the ball with long kicks.

We try to hit high
balls with our heads.
It is not easy.
We wear shin guards
to protect our legs.

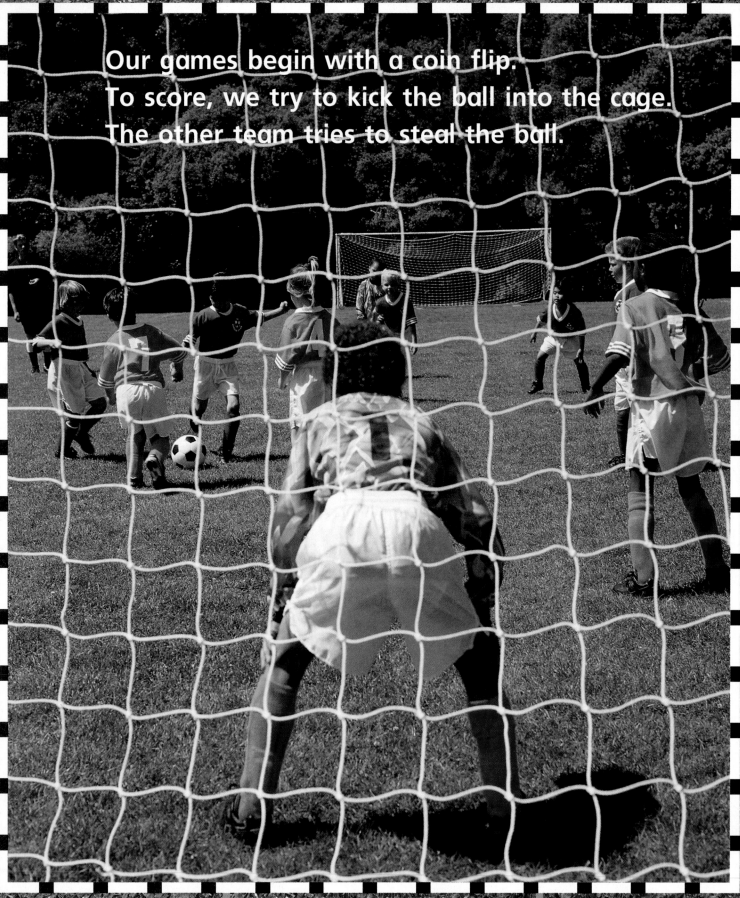

Our games begin with a coin flip.
To score, we try to kick the ball into the cage.
The other team tries to steal the ball.

At half time we
enjoy our oranges.
The coach gives us
some help.
During the game, she
cheers for the team.

143

Sometimes soccer hurts!

But most of the time it is a lot of fun.
The game is over.

We cheer the other team.
Soccer players are proud.
Our game is hard and fast and fun.

146

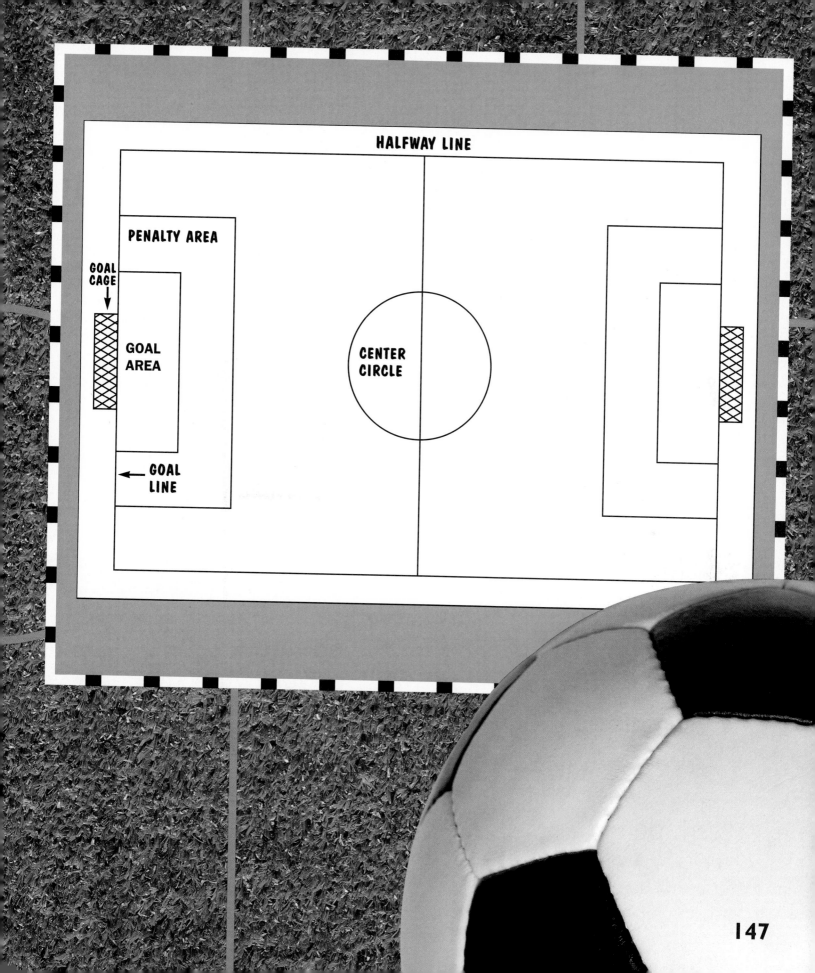

HALFWAY LINE

PENALTY AREA

GOAL
CAGE

GOAL
AREA

CENTER
CIRCLE

GOAL
LINE

147

Glossary

basketball
a game played with a large, round ball by two teams
People can play **basketball** all year long.

coach
a person who teaches people how to play a sport
A football **coach** knows all the rules of football.

coconut
the large, round fruit of a palm tree
A **coconut** has a hard shell and sweet white meat inside.

coconut

enemies
people who hate each other
It's much better to be friends than **enemies**.

hammer
a tool that is used for hitting nails
Dad used a **hammer** when he hung the picture on the wall.

hammer

help
to do something that is useful and needed
Please **help** me get this knot out of my shoelace.

kick
to hit with your foot
To play soccer, the players **kick** the ball.

overalls
pants that have a bib
Painters wear **overalls** when they work.

sprouts
tiny new growths from seeds
The **sprouts** grew into new leaves.

overalls

vegetables
plants whose roots, leaves, or other parts are used as food
My favorite **vegetables** are peas and corn.

vegetables

149

Authors and Illustrators

Jose Aruego pages 74-102

You can tell that Jose Aruego has a great sense of humor just from the pictures he draws. His funny animal characters can be found in many popular books, such as *Whose Mouse Are You?* and *Look What I Can Do!* Sometimes Jose Aruego works on his art with a partner. He has teamed up with Ariane Dewey to do the pictures for *Herman the Helper.*

Nancy Carlson pages 106-134

Bunnies are not the only ones who love sports! Nancy Carlson runs, hikes, swims, and rides her bicycle whenever she can. Most of the characters Carlson draws are funny animals. She even wrote a book about a pig who likes to play football. Other books include *Bunnies and Their Hobbies* and *I Like Me!*

Read Together!

Lois Ehlert pages 10-39

When Lois Ehlert was little, her parents saw that she liked art. They gave her a special table to work at. She cut and pasted. She painted and sketched. That table has traveled with her throughout her career as an artist. She still uses it when creating new art for such award-winning books as *Planting a Rainbow* and *Color Zoo*.

Angela Shelf Medearis pages 40-54

Angela Shelf Medearis is a writer who is always full of ideas for new books. She has written folk tales such as *The Singing Man*, rhyming stories such as *Picking Peas for a Penny*, and realistic stories such as *Big Mama and Grandma Ghana*. She has even written two cookbooks.

Acknowledgments

Grateful acknowledgment is made to the following sources for permission to reprint from previously published material. The publisher has made diligent efforts to trace the ownership of all copyrighted material in this volume and believes that all necessary permissions have been secured. If any errors or omissions have inadvertently been made, proper corrections will gladly be made in future editions.

Cover: © Nicole Katano for Scholastic Inc.

Interior: "Growing Vegetable Soup" from GROWING VEGETABLE SOUP by Lois Ehlert. Copyright © 1987 by Lois Elhert. Reprinted by permission of Harcourt Brace & Company.

"Harry's House" from HARRY'S HOUSE by Angela Shelf Medearis, illustrated by Susan Keeter. Copyright © 1994 by Scholastic Inc.

"Sione's Talo" from SIONE'S TALO by Lino Nelisi, illustrated by Elspeth Williamson. Text copyright © 1992 by Lino Nelisi. Illustrations copyright © 1992 by Elspeth Williamson. Reprinted by permission of Ashton Scholastic Ltd., New Zealand.

"Herman the Helper" from HERMAN THE HELPER by Robert Kraus, pictures by Jose Aruego and Ariane Dewey. Text copyright © 1974 by Robert Kraus. Illustrations copyright © 1974 by Jose Aruego and Ariane Dewey. Used by permission of the publisher, Simon & Schuster Books for Young Readers, Simon & Schuster Children's Publishing Division.

"We Go Together" from Scholastic News, September 30, 1988. Copyright © 1988 by Scholastic Inc. Reprinted by permission.

"Bunnies and Their Sports" from BUNNIES AND THEIR SPORTS by Nancy Carlson. Copyright © 1987 Nancy Carlson. Used by permission of Puffin Books, a division of Penguin USA Inc.

"Rope Rhyme" from HONEY, I LOVE by Eloise Greenfield, illustrated by Diane and Leo Dillon. Text copyright © 1978 by Eloise Greenfield. Illustrations copyright © 1978 by Diane and Leo Dillon. Reprinted by permission of HarperCollins Publishers.

Text from "Soccer Is Our Game" from SOCCER IS OUR GAME by Leila B. Gemme. Copyright © 1979 by Regensteiner Enterprises, Inc. Reprinted by permission of Children's Press, Chicago.

Cover from THE DOORBELL RANG by Pat Hutchins. Illustration copyright © 1986 by Pat Hutchins. Published by William Morrow & Company, Inc.

Cover from LOVING by Ann Morris, photograph by Ken Heyman. Photograph copyright © 1990 by Ken Heyman. Published by Lothrop, Lee & Shepard Books, a division of William Morrow & Company, Inc.

Cover from SEVEN BLIND MICE by Ed Young. Illustration copyright © 1992 by Ed Young. Published by Philomel Books, a division of The Putnam & Grosset Book Group.

Cover from SHOES FROM GRANDPA by Mem Fox, illustrated by Patricia Mullins. Illustration copyright © 1989 by Patricia Mullins. Published by Orchard Books.

Cover from SWIMMY by Leo Lionni. Illustration copyright © 1963 by Leo Lionni. Published by Alfred A. Knopf, Inc.

Cover from THIS IS BASEBALL by Margaret Blackstone, illustrated by John O'Brien. Illustration copyright © 1993 by John O'Brien. Published by Henry Holt & Company, Inc.

Cover from THE TURNIP: AN OLD RUSSIAN FOLKTALE by Pierr Morgan. Illustration copyright © 1990 by Pierr Morgan. Published by Philomel Books, a division of The Putnam & Grosset Group.

Photography and Illustration Credits

Selection Opener Photographs by David S. Waitz Photography/Alleycat Design, Inc.

Photos: 2 bc: © Maryellen Baker for Scholastic Inc.; bc: © Tony Savino for Scholastic Inc.; tc: © Maryellen Baker for Scholastic Inc. p. 3 br: © Maryellen Baker for Scholastic Inc.; ml: © Maryellen Baker for Scholastic Inc. pp. 8-9 c: © Francis Clark Westfield for Scholastic Inc. pp. 41-54: © Ana Esperanza Nance for Scholastic Inc. p. 55 bc: © Lawrence Migdale. pp. 56-57: © Nicole Katano for Scholastic Inc. p. 103 c: © Mickey Pfleger for Scholastic Inc. pp. 104-105: © Nicole Katano for Scholastic Inc. pp. 136-137 c: © Tony Savino for Scholastic Inc.; p. 136 bl: © Tony Savino for Scholastic Inc.; ml: © Maryellen Baker for Scholastic Inc. pp. 138-139: © Halley Ganges for Scholastic Inc. p. 138 bl: © Halley Ganges for Scholastic Inc. p. 139 c: © Ana Esperanza Nance for Scholastic Inc.; tl: © Grant Huntington for Scholastic Inc.; tr: © Grant Huntington for Scholastic Inc. pp. 140-141: © Halley Ganges for Scholastic Inc.; c: © Grant Huntington for Scholastic Inc. p. 140 bl: © Grant Huntington for Scholastic Inc.; tc: © Grant Huntington for Scholastic Inc. pp. 142-143: © Halley Ganges for Scholastic Inc. p. 142 c: © Grant Huntington for Scholastic Inc. p. 143 br: © Grant Huntington for Scholastic Inc.; tl: © Grant Huntington for Scholastic Inc. pp. 144-145: © Halley Ganges for Scholastic Inc.; bc: © Grant Huntington for Scholastic Inc. p. 144 tl: © Grant Huntington for Scholastic Inc. pp. 146-147: © Halley Ganges for Scholastic Inc. p. 146 c: © Grant Huntington for Scholastic Inc. p. 148 tr: © Steve Barnett/Gamma Liaison. p. 149 br: © Ken Reid/ FPG International Corp.; tl: © Dick Luria/ FPG International Corp.; tr: © Stephen Ogilvy for Scholastic Inc. p. 150 bl: Courtesy of Scholastic Trade Department; br: © Mark LaFavor. p. 151 bl: © Lillian Schultz; br: © Bob Daemmrich for Scholastic Inc.